Sorrow

to

Shero

"Some events can leave an unbearable pain so deep that it pierces the soul and changes the essence of our being."

~ Dr. Jeannita Bussle

Sorrow

to

Shero

PAIN, POWER, and PEACE

Dr. Jeannita Bussle

Shero Management, LLC

©Copyright 2020 by Dr. Jeannita Bussle

Publisher: Shero Management, LLC

Cover/Interior Photographs by NLG Photography
Cover/Interior Design: Mystic Circle Books & Designs, LLC

ISBN: 978-0-9999068-0-4 (Paperback)
ISBN: 978-0-9999068-2-8 (Hardback)
ISBN: 978-0-9999068-1-1 (eBook)

Library of Congress Control Number: 2020907941

Dedication

This book is dedicated to my children, RJ and Jordyn; my mother, Toni Clark; and my late father, Arturo Clark.

To my sweet RJ and Jordyn: Everything I do is because of you. You both have changed me and given me the strength I needed. You have been here with me through it all. Although you both were young when these events unfolded, I know you were paying attention. My prayer is that one day, you will be proud of your mother's strength. I want to be someone that you can look up to. I want to be your highest role model, the way your Nana was for me. I love you both.

Mommy, there are no words. I do not know where I would be without you, especially at this point in my life. Everything good in me I learned from watching you, especially the act of forgiveness. God knew exactly what he was doing when he assigned me to you. I love you with everything in me. You are my very best friend.

To my late father; Daddy, I have been strong just like you taught me. I never forgot our many conversations. I learned life from you: you taught me about the streets, men, and how cruel this world can be. You never lied. Your raw and unfiltered truths made me tough. You made me strong because you knew I needed it. I miss you so much, Daddy. I know you are looking down at me smiling and proud.

Acknowledgments

I would like to thank my heavenly father for keeping me. There is no doubt that without Him I would not be here. He is everything to me.

To My Village:

Alicia, Cynthia, Tracy, Monique, Rochelle, Griffin, Ron, Charlotte, Lamonica, Latisha, Ayanna, Brigette, Tammi E, Tammi M, Dionne, Curtis, Uncle Keith, Aunt Maria, Melanie, Judy, Shauni, Demonica, Debra, Donald, Teresa, Eunice, Keisha, Frank, and Charita.

THANK YOU FOR EVERYTHING!
I love you all!

Lastly, I would like to thank Anita Dickason for helping me bring my vision to fruition.

Table of Contents

Introduction

Many little girls fantasize about what their adult lives will be like. As a young girl, I was certainly no exception, and I had everything figured out for my life. I would graduate from college, marry the man of my dreams in a lavish fairy tale wedding, and have at least two children, a boy and a girl to be exact. My imagination allowed me to dream the perfect life for myself, without any heartache. I had it all mapped out. My life was going to be picture perfect. As an adult woman, most of what I dreamed of for my life did occur. Unfortunately, these events did not unfold without heartache.

I struggled with the decision to write this book because I would have to relive painful memories. We live in a society of secrecy and being transparent comes with judgement and ridicule. I decided that if I shared my story, I would be completely honest and not hold back when it comes to my own shortcomings. Transparency is empowering, therefore, it was most important for me to let others facing similar obstacles know they are not alone; as a result, I decided it was time to share my testimony.

Some events can leave an unbearable pain so deep that it pierces the soul and changes the essence of our being. It is when we experience this type of sorrow, that we learn who we really are. My hope is that this memoir will remind people that the tragedies of life can happen to anyone and at any time, however God is ever-present. I am unapologetic in my belief that God is the reason why I am still here. May each person reading my story grow in their faith and continue to dream.

"Your story is what you have, what you will always have. It is something to own."

~ Michelle Obama

One

My Friend and I

As a child growing up in Detroit, I had internal struggles I never shared. Feeling accepted by others and like a failure were two of the many challenges I faced.

Although I was extremely sensitive on the inside, my environment taught me to put on a tough exterior. It is true that some events never leave your memory, regardless of how long ago they occurred.

While in elementary school, I remember my mother waking me up in the middle of the night because a man was attempting to kick our door in. She yelled for me to "get up and run upstairs now!"

We had a metal gate installed that would lock us in during the attempt. My mother called the police, but they didn't show up until the next morning. My uncle ended up coming, but by the time he arrived the individual was gone. I wished my Dad was there but he was working out of state at the time. I can remember thinking as a child that the police did not care about us.

I remember another instance when my neighbor's house was surrounded and shot up late at night. I was asleep upstairs, but woke up and immediately hit the floor. My mother ran upstairs to be with me until the ordeal ended. Although I was used to hearing gunshots sporadically in my neighborhood, this was the closest I had ever been to them. I remember the police taking forever to show up then as well. I never really discussed my feelings, but I always watched what was happening around me.

Middle school was a difficult time in my life. Like so many other teenagers, the transition from childhood was rough. My mother decided to move me from my neighborhood school to a magnet school for gifted students the summer before my sixth-grade year. I absolutely hated that school and I did not want to be there.

During this time, my father was on trial for attempted murder, and I had to testify in his defense. I can still remember the day my mother received a call that my father had been arrested at his job. I was a "Daddy's girl," so the thought of my father being sent to prison terrified me beyond my wildest imagination. Going with my mother to bail my father out of jail taught me as a young girl that life does not discriminate; anything can happen to anyone.

Prison was not foreign to me, as I had been with my parents to visit other family members on more than one occasion. I could handle visiting uncles and cousins in prison, but the reality that one day I could be visiting my own father in prison horrified me.

I had always been a straight A student but my grades began to plummet. I kicked into survival mode because I felt as though I was being targeted for absolutely no reason by the kids at my new school. I found myself in constant girl drama and fights. I never realized how much this event affected me and molded my way of thinking until I was an adult. Instead of focusing on excelling at school, I was constantly haunted of the idea that my father could be sent away.

When I look back, I see that my mother made the right decision in moving me to a school that challenged me academically. I was upset with her at the time, but she did what she knew was best for me. I learned resiliency during this time.

I did not want to add additional stress on my parents, so I did all that I could to improve my grades. This time also pulled me even closer to my friends from my neighborhood, who were more like family. I was able to talk to them about my innermost feelings.

My mom saw my potential and she knew that I was not being challenged by remaining in my comfort zone. Initially, I struggled socially but I gained one of my closest friends to this day because of that move. Most importantly, I was prepared academically for the magnet school I would attend over the next four years.

By the grace of God, my father was eventually found not guilty of all charges pressed against him. His case taught me two valuable lessons that I never forgot: that one event can change your life and that anyone can flip at any moment.

High school was much easier for me socially, but I still suffered deep wounds. I experienced my first heartbreak when my boyfriend at the time had a child with a girl from his neighborhood, completely unbeknownst to me. My father always taught me not to be too trusting of anyone, so although I was hurt I was not surprised.

In August of 1999, I was elated to gain acceptance to Tennessee State University in Nashville. As an eighteen-year-old freshman from Detroit, I saw this opportunity as a way to gain the ultimate historically black university experience, meet friends from across the United States, and to most importantly, find myself.

Tennessee State University had a beautiful campus. I had never seen so many gorgeous, young, educated African Americans in one setting before. I knew immediately that I wanted to get involved in campus culture somehow. I decided to run for Miss Freshman Tennessee State Campus Queen. The current Miss Tennessee State University was the most beautiful woman I had ever seen - both inside and out. She was highly respected by the student population. I desired to learn leadership from her and represent my freshman class.

I won first runner up in the competition. To most people this would not have been a big deal, but as someone that struggled with self-esteem issues, it was personal to me. I understood the loss as failure. My accomplishments at Tennessee State were supposed to prove my haters back home wrong. I clearly needed to heal old wounds because my motives for joining the competition were wrong to begin with.

During this same time, my boyfriend at the time and I began to have problems. I was smothering him with my emotional needs. Additionally, I believed he was being unfaithful to me. Instead of enjoying all that Tennessee State had to offer, I made him my priority. I relied on him in ways that were unhealthy for both of us considering that we were both kids. Making someone your entire world is never healthy, and I of all people should have known better from what my father had taught me and shown me about men.

He and I broke up during the spring semester of my senior year. I did not take the break up well and went into a depression. My mother tried to pray me out of the depression I had slipped in, but nothing seemed to work. What they didn't understand was that my boyfriend was the one person I felt like myself around. He knew all my secrets; he knew my insecurities, my family history, my hurts and disappointments. Again, in my mind, I felt like a failure and I felt embarrassed.

During my sophomore year at Tennessee

State, I met someone who would change the course of my life. He was big around six foot four inches tall, smart, and super funny. The fact that he was from Chicago was a plus for me, being a Detroit girl. There was something about him that made me feel as though I could tell him anything. At first, I could not stand him. I found him to be annoying, as he would refer to me as "lil light skin." He would effortlessly earn As on extremely difficult engineering and physics assignments while the rest of us struggled. This got on my last nerve.

As time passed and I got to know him in one of our classes together, Reginald Bussle became my close friend and confidant. He was a gentle giant, and he had a soft spot for me.

I eventually switched my major during my junior year, but my friendship with Reggie never changed. He always checked on me. He always wanted to make sure I was good.

After I graduated from Tennessee State in May 2003, I moved back to Detroit to begin my teaching career. I kept in contact with Reg, as he took one additional year to finish his degree. After he graduated in May 2004 with a Bachelor of Science in Electrical Engineering, Reg accepted an engineering position with Bell Helicopter in the Dallas/Fort Worth Area. I was still in Detroit teaching and living at home with my parents. I remember telling Reg that I was unhappy and I wanted more. Although I had enrolled in a master's program at the University of Michigan, I felt like my life was at a standstill.

Over the next few years, Reg and I kept in contact and would talk about any and everything. We knew about each other's dating life and professional aspirations. He became a midnight hour type of friend. He was the person that listened to me when my heart was broken time and time again from falling for the same type of man. Reg encouraged me and pushed me to be better. He got me to understand that I was a prize and that if a man could not see that then I didn't need him anyway.

During the summer of 2006, Reg and I planned a trip to Las Vegas with a few friends from school. It was during this trip that I knew I not only loved him as my friend, but that I was in love with him romantically. I valued our friendship too much to say anything and, anyway Reg was dating someone back in Dallas. I kept my feelings to myself out of the fear of losing my friend and/or damaging our relationship.

Sorrow to Shero

"Love makes people do crazy things.
And not feeling loved can bring people to
the edge of madness."

~ *Jacqueline Simon Gunn*

Two

Our Beginning

July 2007 was an exciting time for me. Although I had gotten laid off from the charter school where I had been teaching for the past few years, I had started doing makeup professionally and I was starting to see the light at the end of the tunnel of the master's program I had started years earlier. My goal was to make a career in education but I also enjoyed makeup and all things fabulous. Working for Clinique and MAC Cosmetics at Nordstrom counters gave me a purpose and something to look forward to as I finished my degree.

I also turned my life over to Jesus Christ.

Dr. Jeannita Bussle

Dating one baller after another proved dangerous, and after the last guy I fell for received time for drug trafficking, I knew that I needed a renewed mind. Some things are just not worth your peace.

Growing up, my parents never struggled but I always wanted more. Men with money were a sign of financial security in my eyes, and I needed God to deliver me from this mindset. I decided to turn my attention totally towards my faith, and it was the best decision I ever made.

Reg was very proud of me and the positive decisions I was making. He couldn't believe that I turned down the offer to hold my boyfriend's Cadillac Escalade while he did his time with the feds a "boyfriend" my parents knew nothing about. To this day I don't know what came over me that gave me the courage to send him that text: "Hey I was just sitting here thinking about you." Reg, a jokester, replied, "I'm sure you are. I'm cute." I replied, "Yes you are. We need to talk." My phone rang, and from that moment forward, everything changed.

Many people thought it was Reg that stepped

towards me. They thought he was the one that poured his guts out. The truth is, it was me. I was the one who fell in love with my best friend. I made the first move. I wanted him and I got him.

Reg would sometimes travel for work. He told me his job was sending him to Huntsville, Alabama for a few days and we decided to meet there the next week. We could meet face to face uninterrupted, and no one would ever know our business. The text messages and calls we made leading up to my Alabama visit were some of the most romantic exchanges I'd ever experienced with a man. I knew that my life was about to change, and Reggie confirmed that. He flat out told me, "I'm going to change your life." He was right. July 18, 2007 arrived in no time. The moment I saw him I knew Reg was not playing with me. He was just as serious as I was. I started to cry.

There was so much I had wanted to say to him since our Las Vegas trip. I just let it all out that evening. He told me that he wished I would have said something in Las Vegas. We decided to keep our new relationship private for a while with the exception of our very close friends and family. Everyone seemed supportive and excited for us. I felt blessed to be with someone who really got me and actually paid attention to me. He was someone that was honest, caring, and loving, and he was definitely no punk. I liked that balance in him.

Although he worked a nine to five job, he did everything big. The gifts started coming almost immediately. I still had a year left until I graduated from the University of Michigan so we had to commute from Detroit to Dallas. It was nothing for Reg to call me on a Thursday and tell me to pack my bags for the weekend. When I would check my email, there would be a first-class e-ticket in my inbox from American Airlines to DFW for the following day. Reggie always had money since I'd known him. He kept a nice ride decked out with TVs and rims. You name it, he had it. I had no idea what being his woman would be like. All I knew is that I loved him. He made it his life's mission to make sure I never regretted the day I sent that text message.

Our first Christmas together, while my friends got perfume and sweaters, I got a fully paid trip to Las Vegas to stay in a suite at the MGM Grand, along with a shopping spree, cash, and then some. Giving was definitely his love language, and the guys I had dated in my past didn't hold a candle to Reg. What made all of this so special was that we were in love and had a friendship that ran deep. He would surprise me in ways that actually meant something - like the time his job sent him to Connecticut for a week, he had a couple days off in between and drove from Connecticut to Detroit just to surprise me as I got off work at Nordstrom. That's the type of love he showered me with.

When he invited me to Chicago to meet his family I knew where our relationship was headed. I took an immediate liking to his cousins, aunts, and uncles. They treated me like family and I could tell they were genuine people. I never felt unwelcomed or uncomfortable in their presence. To this day, their love towards me has been unwavering and for that, I am grateful.

Reggie's mother was a little different. She was cordial, but I could tell something in our interaction was a bit off. From the moment we met, it seemed as if she wanted me to know she was the number one woman in Reggie's life. She claimed to like me, but I could tell she was not genuine like the rest of his family. We exchanged numbers and would text and talk from time to time. I wanted a relationship with her because Reg and I were talking about marriage and I was set to move to Dallas after graduation. As our relationship appeared to grow, I had no doubt that I was going to one day marry the man of dreams and into a family that was not dysfunctional.

My parents instantly loved Reggie. They could sense the love between us and they were in total support of our relationship becoming permanent. My parents looked at our love as an opportunity to gain a son. When Reg proposed to me at my mother's fiftieth birthday party in front of my entire family, it came as no shock that my parents were equally as thrilled as I was. Without my knowledge, Reg had flown up the day before and met with my father to ask for my hand in marriage. I had absolutely no idea he was attending the event. He always found a way to surprise me.

I graduated from the University of Michigan-Dearborn with a Master of Arts in Teaching Secondary Education in the spring of 2008. I was engaged and moving to Texas with a mathematics teaching position already lined up in a highly coveted school district. I was the happiest I had been in a very long time. Things could not have been better. Everything I ever wanted seemed to be manifesting itself right before my eyes. My big move to Texas occurred on July 5, 2008. Reggie had secured a nice two-bedroom apartment for us to begin our new life in the suburb of Mansfield, Texas. Although it was just an apartment, it was ours, and we were together.

Reg and I knew from the start that we wanted a non-traditional wedding. Our thoughts were to save money towards the purchase of our first home rather than go into debt for a wedding. We decided to invite forty of our family and friends on a cruise to the

Bahamas and combine our wedding and honeymoon.

Planning our wedding was easy. I had an experienced travel agent I worked with back in Detroit that coordinated the details for myself, Reg, and the guests accompanying us. After a year of planning, the big week came. All of our guests flew into Orlando to travel to Port Canaveral, Florida. This was my first cruise and I was so excited. My bridal suite was beautiful and my closest friends and family members were there to share in this experience with me. The actual wedding day was set for July 22, 2009. Reggie's birthday was July 21, the same day as our rehearsal, so everything was perfect.

When we arrived for what I thought would be a well-crafted rehearsal coordinated by the cruise line, I was greeted by a poorly constructed sign that simply read *"Jeannita's Wedding."* Once we entered the venue, we waited for a wedding coordinator to arrive, but we were shocked to find that there would be no coordinator. I was embarrassed and infuriated. My friends got me together and I attempted to rehearse everyone for my own wedding. Reg's mom approached me and asked angrily, "Why do we have everyone here if there won't be a rehearsal?" The rehearsal was only supposed to be for the actual wedding party, but for some reason everyone from our party showed up. Reggie's mother acted as if this was her wedding and she was the bride. She complained the entire time about everything, despite the fact that she took no part in the planning process.

That evening I noticed a change in Reggie's behavior towards me. He appeared to be standoffish towards me and annoyed all at the same time. I found him on deck that evening in a quiet corner and I attempted to talk with him. I asked him, "What's going on? Are you ok?" He proceeded to question me angrily about the veil his mother had purchased for me. "Why didn't you just go and get the damn veil from her?! Didn't she ask you to come get it?!" he asked. I was hurt and confused. This was the night before our wedding and I found myself having an argument with my new husband that was initiated by his mother.

I would later find out that Reggie's mother

unleashed her anger on him earlier that day about me. She said I was ungrateful and that Reggie and I were ignoring her. The day of the wedding came and I felt simultaneously excited and sad since things were not turning out the way I had always dreamed they would. Instead of having typical bridal jitters, I was dealing with tension from two of the main people that were there to support me - my husband and his mother.

When my father walked me down the aisle, I was so happy. I cried the entire time and everything I felt the night before went away. This was the moment I had waited for my entire life. Once I saw Reggie tear up, I lost it. When my dad gave me away, Reggie took my hand and told me, "You look beautiful." I knew he meant it, but it was also his way of apologizing for the night before. Other than the preacher calling Reg "Maurice" during the reading of the vows, we had a great ceremony that included an open bar reception.

Reggie fully understood that a man is to leave his father and mother and cleave to his wife. His mother on the other hand, had never been married and simply could not comprehend that I was now the top priority in her son's life.

Reg would oftentimes take his frustrations out on me. Our honeymoon period proved to be very tumultuous. And afterwards, the smallest things would set him off. He would yell at me if he couldn't find something he misplaced and I didn't know where it was. If I ever disagreed with him, no matter the subject, it would turn into a full-blown argument as to why I was wrong and he was right. We were not allowed to have differing opinions. We once had a disagreement while driving. Reggie became angry and sped up, driving erratically as an intimidation tactic. Whenever I would attempt to explain my feelings, Reg would turn everything around on me and I would somehow find myself apologizing to him. He would give me the silent treatment for days at a time if I didn't give him sex exactly when he wanted it (which was rare) or if I didn't prepare a meal the way he wanted. I felt as though I was starting to lose myself.

Reg's mother stopped speaking to him as a

result of him finally standing up to her after our wedding cruise. I then observed an even darker shift in his mood towards me. Although he knew his mother was wrong, he still loved her. He made excuses for her behavior. Whenever we would discuss the issue, it appeared to me that he was defending her at times. During one argument he got so angry with me for verbally attacking his mother that he punched a hole in our living room wall. I was scared to death and hurt over this behavior. Reggie was physically intimidating to me. I could not defend myself toe to toe against him if he ever decided to put his hands on me. I knew in my heart that I was not attacking his mother. I simply stated facts that he didn't like. Although he apologized profusely and swore to me he would never do it again, I promised myself that I would never speak about his mother to him in order to be careful. It became obvious to me that Reggie and his mother had an unhealthy relationship. His mother actually viewed him as her man!

Married life started to become better once we found a good church. We argued like every couple does; however, Reg's explosive temper appeared to be calming. He did not talk to his mother up until we realized we were pregnant. The pregnancy was planned, and it only took one month of trying. I could not believe I was about to be someone's mother.

My pregnancy was smooth for the most part. Reg catered to me and made me feel like a princess up until the point that his mother decided to begin speaking to him again. He had shared the news of our pregnancy with her and she knew that at some point she would need to speak with me. Although I was carrying her grandchild, I held firm that it was my child and that there was no way she would be a part of our child's life without respecting me and staying in her place.

We found out we were having a boy during our second trimester. Reggie immediately began working on the nursery. One evening while working on it, Reggie brought up the need for me and his mother to talk. I had been putting off this topic because I already felt stressed and, his mother was not important to me. Maintaining my peace of mind was my priority and there was nothing peaceful about his mother. I told Reg I would talk to her at some point and he blew up at me. He accused me of dismissing his mother and not being fair to her.

We exchanged words and I walked out of the nursery into the guest room across the hall in an effort to calm the situation. Reggie became so angry that he stormed in behind me and punched a hole in the wall (again). Startled, I tripped over an extra can of paint that Reg had on the floor and landed on my stomach. I became hysterical because I could not feel my baby moving. Reg rushed me to the emergency room at a hospital nearby.

Once we got to ER, the nurse checked my vitals and assured me that all was well with my baby. She then asked Reggie to get me a drink of water. I found this request very bizarre. When Reg left out the room, I quickly realized why the ER nurse asked for him to leave. She asked me if I felt safe at home and if I really did trip over a can of paint. I told her I did feel safe, and shortly after Reggie returned with my cup of water in hand.

Although I told the nurse I felt safe, the reality was that I did not feel safe at all. Here I was, visibly pregnant and, in the hospital because of an argument with my husband. Although I did trip over a can of paint, I wondered if Reggie's fist would ever pound through my face instead of a wall in our home. He had already broken his promise never to repeat this behavior. It was at this moment that I realized I was in an abusive marriage.

Instead of viewing Reg as the issue, I felt like a failure. I vowed to do everything in my power to fix things between us. He was my friend that had seen me through so many ups and downs. I had witnessed my parents go through their own struggles growing up. They went through things that would have ripped most families apart, yet they managed to stay together. My parents also made an effort to keep their personal business private. I decided to follow in their footsteps.

My loyalty to Reg was beyond reproach. I was

loyal to him at the cost of my self-esteem and my dignity. If only I knew then what I knew now, I would have spoken up. I would have told my parents about the hell I was in. No one should feel like they are walking on eggshells in their own home especially a woman pregnant for the first-time and approaching her third trimester.

"Sometimes the strength of motherhood is greater than natural laws."

~ Barbara Kingsolver

Three

New Normal

On May 17, 2010 I met my seven pound, grey-eyed, twin Reginald Lamont Bussle Jr or 'RJ' as we call him. He was born after twenty-two hours of labor at thirty-seven weeks. I had developed pre-eclampsia and had to be induced, but I was still able to have a vaginal birth, which I had prayed for. Reggie and I had attended Lamaze classes, but nothing could prepare me for my actual birthing experience. I was so thankful that my mother had taken a flight to Dallas the night before and was able to hold my hand during the experience. Having her support made me feel safe.

RJ was the most beautiful baby I had ever seen. There are no words to describe how I felt when I actually held him. "Hey mister," I said, crying as I kissed him and pulled him close. It was as if he immediately knew my voice. He looked up at me and a calmness came over his face.

We took RJ home three days after I gave birth and I was so excited to begin my new life as a mother. I had prepared as much as possible for motherhood at home, but reality quickly crept up on me. I had extreme fatigue, which many new mothers experience. Breast-feeding proved to be stressful because RJ would not latch on so I had to pump often. My parents came down from Detroit to help for an entire month. They were a huge blessing to both Reg and I. My father developed an instant bond with RJ, which touched me.

I cried and cried when my parents left to return for Detroit because I would miss them very much, but also because Reggie's mother was coming to visit. By this time, she and I had a brief conversation where she gave me an apology that was clearly not sincere, but rather a check off of her to do list. I allowed her to come to keep peace between Reggie and I, but the thought of her made me sick to my stomach.

I was pleasantly surprised when she arrived. My mother-in-law was cordial and on her best behavior. I still did not trust her, nor did I want her there, but I was exhausted so I welcomed her help. For that one week, it seemed as though she and I could co-exist. Reg even seemed happier that the two most important women in his life were getting along.

In August 2010, I went back to work as a new mom and started a master's degree program to pursue school counseling at Dallas Baptist University. My credits from the first master's I earned at the University of Michigan transferred so I did not have very many courses left to take for completion. Even still, I do not realize how I did it. I was running solely on fumes. RJ did not sleep through the night until he was about ten months old. He would wake up almost every hour on the hour. I would listen to friends and colleagues discuss how their kids slept straight through the night at six months, and I thought to myself, *What am I doing wrong?*

Adjusting to fatherhood was extremely difficult for Reggie. During this time, he had also received his first supervisor position. I would ask him to help me with RJ and he would respond, "I need to sleep," or "You are his primary caregiver." These responses made me resentful and bitter towards him. He acted as if I did not need sleep and as though it was not his job as RJ's father to assist in his well-being and care. Reg forgot that although I was a teacher, I also contributed to the household financially. My parents had instilled in me the importance of being able to always take care of myself. They could see how quickly Reg was climbing the corporate ladder and my father flat out told me, "I don't care how much money he makes; you always go to work." I listened.

RJ began walking and talking right on schedule. As we adjusted to parenthood, our relationship slowly improved. As RJ's first birthday approached, I realized that Reggie had made no mention of his mother in months. I told myself I wasn't going to ask any questions because each time she was brought up the outcome was never good. I prayed that God would reveal to me what was going on. He did exactly that.

One evening as I came home late from class I could hear Reg yelling on the phone with someone that I later found out was his mother, saying, "She is my wife! You just don't get it. She ain't just some girl I'm dating. She's not just some female. She's my wife! If you don't understand that I don't know what to tell you!" I immediately went upstairs to ensure RJ was sound asleep before I checked on Reggie. I knew I was taking a chance by asking, "Do you want to talk about it, honey?" To my surprise, he did.

For the first time, Reggie was completely honest about his mother and her toxic ways. He admitted things to me in that conversation about his mother that will forever remain between the two of us. The sad part is that Reg had spent his whole life blaming his father for his problems, despite the fact that a toxic and unstable mother can be just as damaging to a child. I saw a lot of her ways in Reggie.

I came from an immediate family that believed in talking things out. We were far from perfect but we never swept things under the rug. My parents believed it was important to tackle issues head on. I noticed that whenever Reg would blow up at me, punch a hole in a wall, and give me the silent treatment for days at a time instead of apologizing, he would buy me expensive gifts. His mother was no different. Rather than give a sincere apology, she would send boxes of clothes for RJ, and cards with money for Reg and I. It came as no surprise that she began sending gifts after not seeing RJ for the first eighteen months of his life. This was very odd behavior coming from a woman that claimed she was going to be with her grandbaby when he was born.

May 2012 changed the course of our lives. I took RJ to his two-year-old well-child doctor's appointment with my mother by my side. As all parents know, the doctors ask a series of questions to check for developmental delays or deficiencies. RJ's physical development was excellent, but I noticed that his language was not appropriate for a child his age. When his doctor asked me if he was able to speak at least fifty words I responded, "No."

I noticed that RJ began speaking on schedule, but he then started to lose language between eighteen and twenty months old. He was not speaking in two to three-word phrases. I contacted my nearest early childhood intervention agency to begin treatment for RJ. I also enrolled him in private speech therapy with another agency. It was at this point speech therapy began as a new normal in our lives. To this day, I thank God for the finances to be able to intervene early.

Early childhood intervention provided RJ with a speech therapist, occupational therapist, and case manager. During one particular visit with the case manager she spoke to me and asked if I had ever had him tested for autism. My heart sank, though she only confirmed what I intuited. RJ was a very picky eater, he lined up his toys, and he began to flap his hands. All of those signs in addition to his speech delay led me to believe he was autistic. I contacted the local school district to begin the process for testing, which just so happened to be the school district that I worked for. I felt confident with my child being in their care and with the reliability of their results.

By the time I was contacted with the results of RJ's evaluation a few months later, I had graduated from the school counseling program at Dallas Baptist University and had accepted a school counselor position at the middle school I had taught at for the last four years.

The special education team was so kind to me as they went over the results. When the licensed school psychologist finally told me that my child was autistic, I held my composure until the call ended, but once I hung up, I completely lost all self-control.

I stormed out of my office and went looking for my principal who had become a mentor of sorts to me. The assistant principal came running behind me. I knew she was calling my name, but it was as if

I was having an out-of-body experience and I could not respond. The irony is that when I located my principal, she was in a meeting that was being held for a special needs child. I started pounding on her door like a crazy person. Under normal circumstances this behavior would have gotten me written up or fired, but she could see the urgency on my face. She and the assistant principal quickly pulled me into a vacant bathroom across the hall. My co-counselor, who was also like a mentor to me, found us and entered the same bathroom. I screamed and cried like nobody's business while they prayed for me. To this day each of those women hold a special place in my heart.

RJ being diagnosed with autism changed me. I questioned God. In my mind, I had failed a lot in my life, but this was the ultimate failure. I couldn't even give my husband a normal son. RJ would probably never be the star player on the football field or basketball court, just as Reg's own athletic days were cut short due to injury. I reflected on that day in the ultrasound room when the technician announced, "It's a boy!" I had not seen Reg that happy in a long time. I knew he had big plans for RJ, but now I had to tell him this news. Reg knew that I was having RJ tested, but I think he was in denial. He accepted his speech delay, but when we talked about the possibility of him being autistic, he would brush it off. If I talked about any of the symptoms RJ displayed, Reg would say, "That's just RJ."

To Reggie's credit he handled the news well. In fact, he was more concerned with comforting me. He told me that we would get through it and RJ would be fine. My parents were even more supportive. They bent over backwards to give support and even offered to help us pay for applied behavior analysis therapy if we needed it. RJ's teachers were also supportive. If it were not for them, I do not know where we would be.

In the beginning, it appeared RJ's behavior got worse before it got better. Reg and I hired an ABA therapist to visit his school twice a week and work with him in the classroom. We did all we could for our son. I can honestly say that we were not parents that stood by and did nothing because we were in denial and refused to accept the truth.

Oftentimes in the African American community, we get offended by people trying to place labels on our children. As an educator of black and brown children for fifteen years I can understand this mindset. In the case of my own child, I did not mind the label. I was willing to do whatever it took to help my son be successful in school. Having a label has allowed RJ to have the accommodations and modifications necessary for his success in the classroom.

The truth of the matter is that RJ is autistic. No one is out to get him by giving him this label. It is what it is. What I had to learn was that RJ's diagnosis wasn't about me, it was about RJ. I am not the one that struggles socially, RJ does. I was not the one with the speech delay, it was RJ. I had to get over myself, boss up, and turn my attention towards my son.

RJ is considered high-functioning. He can hold a full conversation and he is the most loving child I have ever encountered and all of his teachers agree. He is a blessing to all those that come in contact with him and he has an innocence that is pure and angelic. His innocence has proven to be both a blessing and a curse because at times he has been a target for bullying because of it. RJ thinks everyone is his friend so Reg and I have had to work with him so he is not so trusting.

We received his diagnosis right around his third birthday. While he was younger, he didn't really have any issues with bullying. In fact, early intervention helped to calm some of his behaviors and his speech began to improve. Although RJ continues to make improvements socially, he still struggles to make friends. Kids can be cruel. This is why it is imperative for parents to discuss bullying with their children, especially bullying of children who are unable to defend themselves.

There were many nights I cried myself to sleep. I would pray to God, begging him to remove this from RJ. God said no. The times I was most affected were when I would see fathers interacting with their sons at church, at a restaurant, or at football practice near the middle school where we live. If I noticed, I knew Reg noticed as well. He never once blamed me directly, but he did tell me that I should've read to RJ more when he was little. He would then go on to say that RJ would be just fine.

I had so many uncertainties about the future of my child. I simply wanted to raise a productive member of society. In my heart I knew that RJ could not be shielded from the world. I would have to allow him to interact with the outside world so that he could learn from his peers.

I took a step of faith and signed him up for swimming and soccer at the local YMCA. He did not enjoy the swimming lessons but he loved soccer. Reg and RJ played together as father and son. I remember when RJ scored his first goal; I thought Reg was going to have a heart attack!

This experience taught me to never put limitations on children. I also learned that adults must put our pride aside and acknowledge when our children have an issue so that we can get them the help that they need and deserve. Now instead of asking God to remove the autism from RJ, I ask God to show me how to love him the way he needs to feel loved.

Sorrow to Shero

*"Those curveballs are always coming –
eventually you learn to hit some of them."*

~ *Queen Latifah*

Four

Life's Curveballs

In October 2013, we realized we were pregnant again. RJ was doing well in school and continuing his various therapies. We were noticing major gains in his development so we decided to expand our family. Reg didn't care about the sex of the baby, but I desperately wanted a girl. During my February 2014 doctor's visit, my wish came true. The ultrasound technician informed us that I was carrying a girl! My mother was there and we both screamed in excitement. Reg just gave me a kiss on my forehead because he knew this was what I wanted.

Although I was excited about our new

addition, I had anxiety about the added responsibility. By this time, Reg had switched companies and received two promotions. He was an engineering manager of a large department and was required to travel at times, leaving me at home with RJ. The new position came with more money, but I could tell Reg felt the stress. He would sometimes work on his laptop for long hours into the evening and not spend very much time with RJ and I.

I was also fearful of my daughter being born with a disability. I asked God to let her be born healthy and without any disabilities or developmental delays. I spent a lot of time in prayer during my pregnancy with my daughter.

My prayers were answered on June 28, 2014 when Jordyn Renee Bussle was born. Princess Jordyn or "Mama" as I call her, was alert and fierce. She is her father's twin and immediately had Reg wrapped around her finger. I believe she was exactly what he needed to soften him a bit.

RJ was thrilled about being a big brother. I believe the new role actually helped his development. He became Mommy's little helper and Jordyn's protector. When I needed a fresh diaper for her, he would say, "I'll get it, Mommy!" and beat me to it.

Everything seemed to be going great. Reg's mom had even popped back into the picture and she and I were cordial when she came to visit. She sent me a box of clothes for Jordyn while I was pregnant and I sent her a text to say thank you.

We ended up making amends and I felt comfortable with her coming to visit once I gave birth. I still didn't trust her fully, but I was at a place in my life where peace had priority. If having peace with her meant that I would have peace with my husband, I was all for it.

Jordyn is the light in all of our lives. My parents, sister, and nephew fell in love with her instantly as well. She does not have any developmental delays, but she would have been loved no less if she did. RJ calls himself her protector, but she actually protects him. They are quite the pair. They look out for each other. God knew exactly what he was doing when he handpicked them to be brother and sister.

In March of every year I would go to Michigan to visit my family. The spring break of 2015 was the start of what would forever change me.

When I arrived, I noticed that my father had a cough. I made a point to speak to my parents every day so I thought this cough was simply a lingering cough from the cold he was getting over. I noticed as the days went by that the cough appeared to get worse. My father lived a very healthy lifestyle. He worked out faithfully at his local gym and made every effort to eat clean. Although he had just turned sixty-one that past January, he didn't look a day over fifty. Him being sick was not the norm.

As my parents dropped me and my kids off at the airport the Sunday following spring break, I got a sick feeling in my stomach. At this point, Dad's cough had turned violent. I made my mother promise to take him to the doctor the very next morning. She did exactly that. My mother called me the next day and said the doctors had given my father antibiotics and had diagnosed him with an upper respiratory infection. I spoke to my father later that evening and noticed that he was still coughing but I just assumed the medicine needed time to kick in.

The following Thursday I received a call from my mother that my father had been admitted to the hospital. He called her at work and informed her that something was wrong. I knew something was terribly wrong when my mother told me that I needed to come home. I left work and called Reg immediately. He was already on his way home and had booked me a flight because my mother had contacted him also. I quickly packed my luggage and attempted to prepare clothes for the kids for the next several days without knowing how long I would be gone.

When I got to the Dallas Fort Worth Airport, I Face-Timed my father. My heart sank when I saw my immediate family gathered around him. When I saw tears in my sister's eyes I started to cry. My father was alert and able to talk. I tried to remain positive but my Dad knew me. He knew I was scared, and I knew that he was worried. We all knew the gravity of this situation. According to the doctors, his heart was weak.

My flight arrived to Detroit around midnight. My cousin picked me up from the airport and rushed me to the hospital. When I arrived, my mother met me at the door and walked me to the ICU room where my father was. To my surprise he was awake and alert. It was as if he was waiting for me. I hugged him, and said, "I'm not leaving Daddy." We had the best conversation.

I was so glad to fly home and have a few more one-on-one conversations with my father while he was still able to speak. I did not return to Dallas until mid-April because my dad passed away on March 31, 2015 from giant cell myocarditis, a rare cardiovascular disorder with unknown causes.

Many people with giant cell myocarditis develop abnormal heartbeats, chest pain and, eventually, heart failure. My daddy survived four heart surgeries in three weeks. His body was strong, but God said, "Enough."

Although I still had Reggie, my daddy was the only man that never broke my heart. Reggie and my father had grown very close over the years, but only because I kept the mental and verbal abuse that I endured a secret. I knew the potential outcome if I had told my father what was happening in my household.

My dad referred to Reg as his son, not his son-in-law. Reg called him Pops. I had to ask my brother-in-law to call Reg the night my dad passed because I could not bring myself to do it. Reg took the news extremely hard. My dad had been the father that Reggie never had.

Explaining all of this to RJ was another beast. My father had an exceptionally close bond with RJ. If you put me, Reg, my mother, and my father in a room with RJ, he would go to Granddad first every time. My dad was hero to all of us and so many others.

Wednesday, April 8, 2015, we held the funeral for my dad in Southfield, Michigan. The chapel of the megachurch my parents attended was packed to capacity. I was moved by the outpouring of love my family received from friends and family. To see the massive crowd was a confirmation that my father was in fact an extraordinary man.

I was shocked when Reggie got up to speak during the remarks section of the program. He told the story of when he flew to Detroit to ask my dad for my hand in marriage. He revealed that my father told him what would and would not be tolerated in terms of how I would be treated.

This story touched me because it felt as if my dad was speaking to me from the grave through my husband in some weird way. The very person who had inflicted emotional damage on me, was standing in front of over one thousand people discussing how my father wanted me to be treated. I was struck by the irony of it all.

At that moment I made the decision to honor my father by demanding respect. I looked at my dad's casket and back at Reggie. In my mind, I knew that I could no longer allow myself to be disrespected and abused. My father respected my mother, and Reggie was going to respect me or we would have to get divorced.

My parents raised me to be strong. I thought about all of the conversations my dad and I had when he would drive me to and from Detroit to Tennessee State University. I thought about everything he and my mother had taught me. I thought about how they sacrificed to put me through school. I thought about my dad beating that case years ago and how God showed up when things didn't look very promising. If God showed up then, he would show up now.

To be completely honest, I had been afraid to leave Reggie. At this point, he had been promoted to Director of Engineering of a major medical supply company and we had just closed on our dream home. I drove a Mercedes. I had every designer bag and shoe on the market and weekly hair and nail appointments. Reggie gave me free range to buy whatever I wanted, whenever I wanted.

At this point, money wasn't a thing for us. Reggie's annual bonus check was more than some people's annual salary. He had exposed me to the good life, and I was afraid to let that go. Many women who are married to powerful, rich men will not admit this, but I will humbly and honestly admit that the money was a big reason I stayed.

History was another reason I stayed. I had convinced myself that Reggie was the same guy from college that grew to be my best friend. I didn't want to start all over with someone else. I told myself that the grass isn't always greener. I wanted my kids to grow up in a two-parent household.

The truth is that Reg and I had good and bad times like every couple. When things were good between us, they were great. After my father's funeral we began dating each other more. His new position required long hours and more travel, but he started making time for me and the kids. My dad's sudden passing helped both of us to realize that time is precious and things can change in an instant. Reg promised to work on his communication, and for a while he did. Life was good for us at times.

However, when things were bad between us, they were extremely bad. Although Reggie's outbursts and mood swings seemed to lessen over time, when he did have them, they were worse than the early years and even more explosive. The difference was that now I was explosive as well.

After my father's funeral I decided that I was no longer going to be Reggie's emotional punching bag. If he popped off at me, I popped right back off and my mouth was vicious. Reggie started to become frustrated when he realized I wasn't the same little girl that he was used to manipulating. His ego had been bruised. I didn't care because as far as I was concerned, he had it coming.

What really set me off was when Reg would turn his anger towards RJ. When he realized he had finally met his match with me, he tried to take out his frustrations on RJ. This is where I turned crazy. One particular time I told him, "You better kill me right now because you will not yell at my son again!" He could see the look on my face and that look said I was willing to die for my son. Reggie would get so easily frustrated with RJ about the smallest things. Around this time RJ was only around six or seven years old. After I showed my crazy, he backed off.

I made excuses for Reggie for far too long. Just

because he grew up in a dysfunctional home and witnessed abuse did not give him the right to treat me the way he did. I felt extremely bad that he had these experiences, but they did not give him a free pass to abuse his wife. Just because Reggie had self-esteem issues regarding his weight did not give him the right to accuse me of flirting with other men he viewed as a threat. It also didn't give him the right to accuse me of wanting to exercise and eat healthy to look good for another man.

Reggie's parents demeaned him, but that did not give him the right to act the same way towards his son, who adored him. It was not RJ's fault that he was born with autism. What type of father would treat their young child like he was embarrassed by them? RJ is extremely attentive and intelligent. Even at times we thought he was not paying attention, he was. Reggie was setting himself up to be resented and hated by RJ the same way he had resented and hated his own father and, in many ways his mother as well. It was up to him to break the cycle.

Sorrow to Shero

"Strength is what we gain from the madness we survive."

~ *Unknown*

Five

August 2017

Saturday, August 19, 2017 began like most weekends in my household. The kids woke up early and I got up with them as Reg slept in. I didn't mind him sleeping because he would usually stay up late working if we had not gone out the night before. Jordyn had her weekly dance class late each Saturday morning and Reg had told me that he was going to take her. I made breakfast in enough time for everyone to eat before it was time for them to leave.

Around 10:30 am I noticed that Reg had still not gotten up so I asked RJ to tell his daddy that breakfast was ready. Reg had fallen asleep upstairs in our media room the night before, which was not at all uncommon, especially on nights he stayed up working. RJ came downstairs and said, "Mommy, he won't get up." I told RJ to go tell him again. RJ came back down the stairs and told me that he still would not get up. At that time, I decided to go upstairs and wake him up myself after I fixed both kids' plates and got them settled at the table.

Once I got upstairs, I found Reg stretched out on the media room floor. I called out to him that his food was ready. What happened next took my breath away and still hurts me today. He sat up and started going off on me like I was a stranger off the street, saying things like, "Dawg, you see I'm sleep!" and "Why the fuck you wake me up!" I had enough of it. He wasn't about to treat me like that any longer. I went smooth off.

I told him that he was not going to treat me that way and that he had me fucked up. He jumped up and began following me down the stairs yelling and carrying on. I couldn't believe this was really happening. Was he really starting off this beautiful Saturday going off on me out of the clear blue just because?

When I noticed RJ and Jordyn looking at us, I realized I could not go on like this. They both looked frightened and that did it for me. I turned around, looked him square in the face, and yelled "I'm done with your ass! I'm getting an attorney! I'm done!"

He backed away from me and got eerily quiet. I stormed off and tried to gather my composure. Reggie followed me into our bedroom and asked me, "Are you serious?" I told him, "Yes. I'm tired of you treating me like this." He kept trying to apologize, but I wasn't trying to hear it. I was done.

This had been a repeated pattern of his. He would blow up at me, expect me to take it - and I would - then he would apologize, and the pattern would repeat. I refused to be his emotional punching bag moving forward, especially in front of my children. They were not going to grow up in dysfunction.

Reggie took RJ and Jordyn to Jordyn's dance class. They returned a little over an hour later, at which point I had calmed down a bit but my mind had not changed. The decision had been made. Reg had RJ came into the bedroom and said, "Mommy, Daddy is sorry."

At that point, it didn't matter who was sorry. My kids and I were leaving. I had heard it all before: "Baby, I'm sorry;" "I love you, honey;" "I won't do it again."

I was just so pissed. The fact that he was trying to use my children to butter me up infuriated me even more.

Reggie came into the bedroom where I was ironing and attempted to talk to me. I basically told him that I wanted us to co-parent like grown adults. I went on to say that I didn't care about the house and that he could have it. I would move back into the apartments up the street that we lived in years ago.

We went back and forth for a little bit with him trying to change my mind but he and I both knew that this time was different. Even he knew that he had crossed the line big time. He could tell in my demeanor that I was serious.

Reg was flying to Chicago the next day to begin a week-long business trip. Before each trip, he always left me cash in the house in case of an emergency. He told me that he was running to the ATM and that he would be right back.

When he returned to the house, he told me he was leaving me some money in his nightstand and going out to the cleaners, and to run a few errands. He then tried to hug me, but I refused. Before he left, Reggie hugged and kissed Jordyn and RJ and told them, "Take care of Mommy. Daddy's about to go and run some errands. I love y'all." At that point, he walked outside, got in his blue Cadillac Escalade, and drove away.

I packed the kids up maybe an hour later and we went to the grocery store. As I completed my shopping and unloaded my groceries from the shopping cart into my trunk, I received the following text from Reggie:

I'm sorry I didn't have the courage to tell you this would be the last time I would see you in this life. Make sure the kids have happy memories of me. I gotta go.

I immediately hurried to get the kids in the car and called Reggie. He didn't answer. I kept calling and calling until I drove the short distance home from the grocery store. There was still no answer. I tried texting him and he finally responded with *I gotta go.* By this time I saw that I had a missed call from his mother. This let me know he had called her and that this was not just some sick joke.

Once I got the kids in the house, I ran into our master closet where Reg kept his gun and realized it was gone. Normally I wouldn't have thought anything about the gun being missing, since he would occasionally go to the gun range, but considering the circumstances I knew I had a decision to make.

I tried Reggie one more time, but this time his phone went straight to voice mail. Reggie knew that I took threats of suicide and insinuations of suicide seriously. He knew that when I was a young teenager, a male friend and former classmate back home in Detroit committed suicide. This situation was absolutely nothing to take lightly, and I did what I thought was best. I called the police. When asked about the nature of my call, I responded, "I believe my husband is suicidal."

The dispatcher asked me for a description of the car, and of my husband. I knew that this was not going to turn out well. This was in the midst of the Black Lives Matter movement when black men and women were being killed by the police openly. Reg was six feet four inches tall, well over three-hundred-fifty pounds, and he was driving a Cadillac Escalade carrying a loaded gun. I had been in the car with Reggie once before when he got pulled over for speeding and I knew his disposition with police officers. Like many African American men growing up in inner cities, he did not trust the police or respect them. To top this off, Reg had a horrible and explosive temper.

By this time, I had contacted his mother and uncle to inform them of what was happening. I had also informed them that I had called the police. I called my own mother to let her know what was happening and she told me that she had received an *I love you* text from Reg earlier. One of his college roommates contacted me and asked if everything was ok because he had received a text from Reg also. He was obviously saying his goodbyes.

Once the officer arrived to my home, I went over all the details of the day. By this time, it had been over two hours since I had last seen Reggie and he could have been anywhere. I located the vehicle identification number for his Escalade from our insurance card and gave that to the officer. He then sent out a statewide search for the car. The officer asked me if I knew if my husband was armed. I knew he was, so I said yes. I made sure to tell the officer that the gun was registered to Reggie. I wanted to ensure that he knew that Reg was not some criminal on the loose. When I heard him get back on his radio and say, "The suspect is armed," my heart sank.

I have often thought about my decision to call the police that day. Growing up in Detroit, I never trusted them, especially after my father's arrest. In this case, I was trying to save my husband's life. I felt that I was damned if I did and, damned if I didn't. If I had not called the police, there would have been those that would have questioned why I didn't do anything. And as the day went on, I would learn that my husband blamed everything that transpired that day on me.

The officer at my home talked with me to figure out why Reggie was suicidal. As we talked, a call came through on his radio relaying that Reg had been spotted in east Texas. He was alive and I was grateful. An officer had spotted him coming out of a gas station and was approaching the vehicle.

Just when the ordeal appeared to be over, the officer at my home and I heard through radio the officer at the scene yell, "The suspect is fleeing!" Instead of complying with the officer's directive to step away from the vehicle, Reggie sped away. Up until this point, he had not broken any laws: the gun he was carrying was registered to him and he had not crossed state lines with it. Now, however, he had disobeyed an officer's order with a gun on him. I would later learn that he had alcohol in the truck.

The officer at my home told me that OnStar had the capability to slow the vehicle so my husband was not going to get very far. I was so distraught and scared. In that moment I knew that this situation was not going to turn out well for anyone. By running from the police, Reggie had already shown he had zero intention of backing out of what he had set out to do. He was on a mission. I just prayed that no one would get hurt trying to stop him. I tried to keep calm so I would not scare RJ or Jordyn who I had sent upstairs to watch cartoons.

I had so many thoughts going through my head, but in my heart, I knew I did the right thing by calling the police. I tried to call Reg again. To my surprise he answered. I begged him to stop this. I told him I loved him. He responded, "No you don't." I told him that the police only wanted to help him and then he hung up on me.

As the officer at my home continued to gather details about what Reg was angry about, he voiced his conclusion, "Basically you told him you were leaving him, and to punish you for it, he is going to kill himself."

By this time, one of my dear friends happened to call me. She rushed over after I told her what was going on. Another friend also came after the first friend called her, so I had support. It had now been at least four hours since Reggie left the house. OnStar had stopped his Escalade and Reggie was now in a police standoff. He was completely surrounded by marshals and police in a place I had never heard of Longview, Texas near the Louisiana border.

During the standoff, I kept calling Reggie. Sometimes he would answer; sometimes he would send me to voicemail. I even had RJ make a video asking, "Daddy come home to play with me." I sent the video but, he wouldn't respond. Hours went by and Reg would not get out of his truck. By this time, local news in east Texas had picked up the story. Traffic had to be diverted off of the freeway because Reggie was now considered "armed and dangerous." He had shot at the police.

Negotiators were called in to try to talk Reggie out of the car. OnStar had the technology to allow his mother to speak with him by phone in an effort to get him out, but Reg kept turning the speaker off. I called him again and when he answered I could hear the police outside of his vehicle yelling at him. I started screaming and begging him to get out the car. He said, "Fuck them! They are not taking me alive!" Then he hung up on me again.

By this time, night was approaching and I realized that the police had been more than patient with Reggie. The original officer that came to my home had left, but I told him about Reggie and who he was. This officer had the capability to communicate on my behalf with the officers in east Texas who were on the scene. These officers knew that Reggie was an engineering executive. They knew he had no criminal record. They knew he was a father. They also knew that I had begged for them not to hurt my husband. Around 8:30pm, I continued to text Reggie words such as, *I love you* and *Please come home.* Around 9:00 pm I received one last message through text from my husband. He told me:

This is all your fault. Thanks for calling the police.

My friends and I were following updates from the Longview news station online that had picked up the story. I had been in contact with negotiators, but after a while they stopped communicating with me. Now the only way I could receive updates was through news outlets. For a while, the story did not change and I was left in the dark. All I could do was pray, but in my heart of hearts I knew what had happened. I hit refresh on my phone one last time and the title I saw read, *Suspect in I-20 standoff is dead.* I found out that my husband was dead online.

"Once you reach deeper and deeper into your reality, you approach closer and closer its surreal essence."

~ *Talismanist Giebra*

Six

Moving On

The officer that came to my home initially came to the right conclusion. I was leaving my husband, and to punish me for it, he killed himself. Police showed up at my home around midnight to deliver news I already knew.

I really didn't know how to feel after I realized that I was now a widow. Sadness was not my first emotion. I was angry and at times I was numb. Rather than go through a divorce like any rational adult, Reggie did in fact punish me. The very person that was once my very best friend and confidant hurt me in a way that only God would be able to heal me from. Reggie was in his right state of mind to tell others in his life that he loved them before taking his life, but as for me, the mother of his children and his wife, he made sure I knew that this was my fault.

It was my fault that he went off on me that morning after I made him breakfast. It was my fault that I didn't simply accept his apology and move on like I always did. It was my fault that I had enough and refused to be a doormat for him. It was my fault that he got his gun and drove to east Texas. It was my fault he fled from police. All of this was my fault. He blamed me all the way to his grave. He never accepted responsibility for his actions. He believed this was my fault and he made sure that I knew.

How was I going to explain this to RJ and Jordyn? What was I going to do? I had so many thoughts go through my mind, but I knew I had to pull myself together for the sake of my children.

One of my friends called my mother to update her. She immediately booked a flight to Dallas for the next day. I decided to wait and tell RJ and Jordyn once she arrived. I needed her presence to have that conversation. I then called Reggie's uncle to update him. I would let him tell Reggie's mother. I told his college roommate who then updated a couple of his close friends.

Once everyone who needed to know what happened was informed, I had to contact Reggie's job. He was supposed to be on a flight to Chicago that Sunday. I sent an email to his immediate supervisor, left my phone number, and asked her to call me immediately. I also looked up a human resource contact at Reggie's company and sent the same email request.

After I sent the emails to Reggie's colleagues I began to panic. Reality hit me and I began to think about finances. Reggie was the breadwinner for our family. I feared I would lose everything. Although he was very responsible and had policies set up, I knew what was said about insurance money and suicide. Although Reggie's death involved the police, would it still be considered a suicide?

I was confident that my kids and I would be okay based on what I knew I had in my possession and based on what I knew we would receive from his job, but I did not know to what extent our lives would be altered. I was in a state of shock and disbelief. So many thoughts were going through my mind. I needed to feel confident that I could provide for and raise my two small children.

I remembered Reg giving me instructions on what to do if anything ever happened to him. I had his security codes to files that I knew I would need. I began printing off documents that I had access to. At this point, I was in full survival mode - not just for my sake, but for the sake of RJ and Jordyn.

The next morning friends flooded my home. I had watched my mother go through the process of burying my father so I knew I would need all the help and support I could get. When I picked my mother up from the airport, I felt a sense of relief. My mother's presence always gave me comfort. She knew exactly what to do to help me and she could relate to my feelings.

After my friends left Sunday evening, it was

time for me to tell RJ and Jordyn. At this time, they were only seven and three years old. They knew something was wrong and they had been asking, "Where is Daddy?" With my mother by my side I had to look my children in their innocent faces and tell them, "Daddy is in heaven. He is not coming home." To my surprise, they did not cry or have a breakdown. They said, "Ok Mommy," and each gave me a hug and kiss. I believe they did not fully process what I was saying to them at that time, but I knew grief counseling was inevitable.

An article was published in the Longview, Texas newspaper a couple days later. Up until this point Reggie's identity had been concealed, and now it was public knowledge. I felt sick to my stomach. Although Reggie had caused a huge and unnecessary inconvenience by shutting down the highway, there was no reason his name needed to be published. My son shares his father's name. I know how cruel kids can be. Now when RJ gets older, if he ever decides to look up his own name, there is a possibility that this article will pop up. I could not focus on that because I had a funeral to plan.

Reggie and I never discussed where each of us would be buried. As his wife and next of kin, that decision was left up to me and me alone. I made the decision to fly his body back to Chicago. His family said they would understand if I held the funeral services in Texas, but I believed that burying him in Chicago was the right thing to do.

I had to go to a morgue in Dallas to collect Reggie's wallet, cellphone, and keys before his body was flown off to Chicago. I was met by a deranged individual that looked like a character from a horror movie. I was handed blood stained keys, a blood-stained wallet, and a blood-stained cellphone that belonged to my husband. The whole scene felt surreal.

I spoke with several of Reggie's family members leading up to the day the kids and I were set to arrive in Chicago. I knew that Reggie had a troubled upbringing, but even more details were revealed to me during this time. One family member even admitted to me that there were things that should have been addressed when Reggie was a child that never were addressed. When I began to describe Reggie's temper, his family was not surprised. In fact, I was told that Reggie had punched holes in the wall of his grandmother's house. I was furious. It seemed as though everyone knew that Reggie had a problem all along.

I dreaded having a conversation with Reggie's mother once I landed in Chicago, but I knew it was coming. I hated to have my children in an environment that could potentially be hostile. When she and I finally had a moment alone to talk, I expected her to blame me, but she didn't. Instead she told me that she knew Reggie had a bad temper. She said she remembered him punching holes in walls as a young teenager and that Reggie's father had treated her the same way that I had been treated. I guess that was her way of trying to connect with me.

When I spoke to Reggie's dad, he was definitely not surprised by anything I said. In fact, he flat out asked me, "Did Reginald ever hit you?" When

I answered no, he was stunned. He went on to tell me that Reggie got his temper from him, almost as if it was a badge of honor. I was disgusted.

As far as I was concerned, my husband never stood a chance with parents like the ones he had. Although I was still very angry at Reg, my eyes were opened. I did not excuse Reggie's actions, but a lot of things made better sense to me. I now understood why he never brought his kids to Chicago. RJ had visited one Christmas when he was a baby and Jordyn had never been up until now. I hated that her first visit to Chicago was because I had to bury her dad.

I was completely livid with my in-laws. What type of parents wouldn't help their child when they need it? Were they that damaged themselves that they completely overlooked their son's needs? Were they so messed up themselves that they never thought to get Reggie counseling? The fact remained they did nothing.

I began to think about all that Reggie and I had done for RJ as soon as we found out about his diagnosis. What type of parents would we had been if we had done nothing to help him? Children do not know that they have an issue. They are living in their reality whether that reality is considered normal or not. It is up to the adults around them to get them the help they need.

Reggie's viewing and funeral were held at a funeral home in Chicago. I was grateful for the outpouring of support that I received. Reggie's extended family was awesome as well. To this day they have a special place in my heart because they never once passed judgement. In my presence, they have always been kind, loving, and encouraging. They displayed this love for me during this very difficult time.

During Reggie's funeral I had moments of anger. I stood over my husband's casket and tried to process what I was looking at. The funeral home did a great job of ensuring Reggie looked like himself, but I could still see a small drop of dried blood on his ear. I envisioned Reggie in his final moments and I wondered what was he thinking. Was he afraid? Did he pray? What was going through his mind before he pulled the trigger? I was angry over the fact that I was burying my husband at thirty-six years old. I was angry because my children were going to grow up without their father.

This reality hit me even harder when I saw pictures of Reg with RJ and Jordyn on a projector screen during the family hour. What hurt the most is that Reggie did this to RJ and Jordyn. He didn't die in a car crash or from a heart attack. He did this to our kids and to me. Reggie and I had discussed many times over the years the importance of having two parents in a home. He wanted for RJ and Jordyn what he never had.

In no way do I feel that if Reggie had died of another cause the pain would have been easier, but the fact that he was the one that inflicted all of this pain upon us was a hard pill to swallow. I was certainly not a traditional grieving widow.

My demeanor was also standoffish at times towards Reggie's parents. Understandably, they were upset and it showed during the services, but I still had a hard time feeling sympathy for them. When

Reggie's mother began weeping and screaming over his casket, I stood to the side and had flashbacks of all the times Reg would be visibly hurt when discussing her with me. I thought about how hurt he was when his mother didn't speak to him for the first eighteen months after RJ was born and how I had watched him attempt to reach out to her on multiple occasions. I thought about her telling him through email, *You are not a man.* Her yells may have moved the other members of the audience, but they did absolutely nothing for me.

I felt even less emotion for Reggie's father. As I stood to the side and watched him scream over the casket, I pictured Reggie as a little boy on the front porch waiting on his father to show up, though he never did. I thought about the conversations Reggie had with me where he talked about seeing abuse in his home.

Reg's father didn't know that in one of the text messages he sent me during the police standoff, Reggie indicated that he felt he was becoming more and more like his father and that was his greatest fear.

Dr. Jeannita Bussle

I have never been good at hiding how I really feel, so I was glad when everything was over. I felt a huge sense of relief. I was excited to get back home to Texas, wipe away my tears, and move on with my life.

Sorrow to Shero

"Every man has a right to be wrong in his opinions. But no man has a right to be wrong in his facts."

~ *Bernard Baruch*

Seven

The Hard Truth

A lot has been said about me and my marriage to Reggie since he passed away. It is so true that when people don't know your story they will speculate. People will tell your story with confidence and boldness, as if it is the gospel, without having any facts to back up the details. It has been said that I was a gold-digger that only married Reggie for his money. I have heard that my husband was a drug kingpin and this was all a "death before dishonor" cover-up. Reggie's father even had the nerve to ask me if RJ was really Reggie's son and if that was that the real reason Reggie was so upset that day. The list goes on and on.

The gold digging comments are laughable to me. I know in my heart what my relationship was with my husband. I was not a groupie that met a young engineering executive and got pregnant. I was the same girl that met Reggie when we were both nineteen-year-old sophomores at Tennessee State University. I was the same girl that shared a two-bedroom apartment with Reggie when I first moved to Texas after we got engaged. I drove a Ford Mustang and he drove a Chevy Avalanche back then. Reg was an individual contributor and had not even earned his first supervising position yet.

There is a popular saying that goes: *keep that same energy*, and I totally agree. It is important to keep that same energy when remembering that I was there from the very beginning and remained solid every step of the way, even at times that I should have left. It is important to keep that same energy and remember that I was the one that stood by his side through the ups and downs and through every rejection and promotion. It is important to keep that same energy when remembering that oftentimes I was a single parent while Reggie traveled. I never complained, yet I encouraged him, and he excelled to become a director of engineering by thirty-five years old.

I laugh because I know that I was not Reggie's downfall. My husband had issues that should have been addressed long before we ever met. In fact, I later found out that Reggie's jealous and controlling tendencies were a pattern. The start of my healing process was accepting that none of this was my fault.

When Reggie's body was pulled from his Cadillac Escalade the police discovered what they described as "a large amount" of cash. For as long as I've known Reggie, he always carried money on him. For him to have a four-figure amount of cash at any given time was nothing out of the ordinary. That was just who he was. What the police were considering a large amount was very subjective. I knew that to Reggie, the dollar amount was nothing. It was also nothing to me.

When the police questioned me about this, I

told them just that. They had no evidence of illegal activity from Reggie and they had nothing to charge me with. I was given every single dollar Reggie had on him that night. As the money was handed over, I could see blood on some of the one-hundred-dollar bills. The investigation was closed.

What I knew for a fact was that my husband hustled to provide for his family. What I witnessed was a young man that rose to the top quickly. The man I loved had two master's degrees in engineering from Southern Methodist University. I personally watched Reggie go to work every single day for the 10 years we were together and handle his business.

When Reg passed, I attempted to give his father a chance. I had always thought that Reg was too hard on his father and that his mother had poisoned his mind against his dad. Reggie's dad never met Jordyn and he had only seen RJ once during Christmas years ago. When the kids and I arrived for Reggie's funeral, his aunt and uncle picked us up and took all three of us to see Reggie's dad.

Reggie was an only child, and my father-in-law cried and thanked me for allowing him to spend time with his grandchildren. He and I kept in touch for several months after Reggie's funeral. It was through Reggie's dad that I gained even more insight into some of what Reggie had experienced growing up. Although I did not trust his father because of my conversations with Reggie, I appreciated his father's honesty. At least he was willing to admit where he had gone wrong in his relationship with his son, whereas, Reggie's mom pretended that she was a saint of a mother. His dad was very transparent and let me know that both he and Reggie's mother had a part to play in what Reg experienced growing up.

I was shocked when my father-in-law questioned me about RJ being Reggie's son. I was confused and very hurt. He and I had so many conversations about Reggie, his temper, and his childhood during the months following the funeral and by now it was apparent to all those that knew Reggie personally that I was not to blame. To some people, they would rather make up a bold-faced lie than accept the truth. Just because we may not like the truth or because we have a hard time processing it, doesn't mean it changes. Some people cannot handle the truth even when it's obvious.

What I could not understand was that all those that knew Reggie up close and personal were able to describe his temper in great detail. What I described came as no shock. The police officer that came to my home that August day was right: I was leaving my husband and to punish me for it, he killed himself.

It takes a mean and malicious person to carry out such an act, but it is what it is. I started to put the pieces together. Reggie never took off his wedding ring, but he left it in one of our guest rooms on the dresser that August day. He propped it up in the original case before he drove off. I hadn't noticed but one of my friends saw the ring when she came to the house the next day to help me. Reggie wanted me to see it. The money that he told me that he was leaving in the nightstand turned out to be $10,000 cash in an envelope. He knew I would need access to cash in the days and weeks following his death so he ensured I had it. Reggie kept a safe that I always had a hard time opening. This safe contained important information that would be needed for emergencies. The next day I discovered that Reggie had the safe already opened for me. My husband had time to think this through before he got in that Escalade. He had plenty of time to change his mind, but he didn't. This was going to happen. It was just a matter of when.

After I cursed my father-in-law out, I sent him a screenshot of the text message that Reggie had sent me during the police standoff where he stated he was becoming like his father and that his greatest fear was to be anything like him. I told Reggie's father to go and choke on the bottle as he thought about his son's final words. After that, I never heard from him again.

Up until this point, I had always been respectful to my father-in-law, but all gloves come off if someone mentions one of my kids. Jordyn is a spitting image of her father, while RJ looks more like me and my side of the family. That was the bottom line and the entire justification for why my father-in-law questioned me. He tried to say that I only sent pictures of Jordyn to him, however, that was completely false. He needed to be glad that I sent pictures of my children at all because their father, his son, refused to allow the kids to have any contact with him at all. I even encouraged Reggie to make peace with his father on more than one occasion, and he turned on me in an instant. I shouldn't have been surprised because, once again, my father had always taught me that anyone can flip at any moment.

Some may say that sending Reggie's father that screenshot was malicious but I did not care. Now that he was looking for answers he had them. I not only sent his dad the screenshot, but I added Reggie's mother to the same message. They both were able to see Reg discuss how he felt he had been punished by God since he was a child. These screenshots could not be refuted because the police had included them in their investigation. It was what it was and my former in-laws had to deal with it. RJ or I were not going to be used as a scapegoat for anyone. Since they were looking for answers, now they had them. Reggie's parents had to accept their own son's final words.

I have often thought about what I could have done differently in my marriage. For the longest time, I allowed my husband to speak to me any way he wanted and whenever he wanted. I always tried to pick my words carefully in an effort not to anger him. Although I have no regrets for finally standing up for myself, I wish that I would have kept my composure instead of cussing and fussing at Reggie simply because he was doing the same to me.

There is no guarantee that the outcome would be any different regardless of how I responded to being cursed out that morning. I have asked myself if Reggie would have responded better to me announcing that I wanted a divorce if I was calm. Would he had allowed me to simply pack my things and leave with my children? Would we had been able to co-parent in peace like two civilized adults? I have thought about the answer to these questions repeatedly and I am simply unsure of the answers.

I am so happy that my final words to my husband were those of love. Although he was angry at me that August day, I am the only person that he would actually hold a conversation with during the police stand-off.

I remember telling him how much I loved him and how I always loved him. He never said it back, but I know he heard me.

As I spoke to him, I could hear the police on loudspeakers calling his name. Through the screams I told Reggie that he was an awesome father, that we all needed him, and that he changed my life for the better.

It is because of Reggie that I am the mother of two beautiful children. When I am asked would I do it all over again, my answer is always yes. Without Reg, I would not have RJ and Jordyn, as they are my greatest joy. I cannot imagine my life without them.

I learned a lot from Reggie. He taught me about money, investing, home ownership, and staying out of debt. I purchased my first two homes with Reg. I also buried my father with Reg by my side. I traveled with Reg, attended concerts with Reg, and had many quiet evenings at home with my Reggie.

As I look back, I realize that my husband needed professional help. We had the best times when he was the big funny guy I met at nineteen years old, but he could suddenly change in an instant. As I started to speak to more professionals, I now realize I was married to a man with mental illness. Whether he had emotional and/or anger disturbances, bipolar disorder, or both, there was something clearly wrong.

Literature that I have read describes bipolar disorder as a mental health condition that causes extreme mood swings. These extreme mood swings can affect a person's sleep, judgment, behavior, and their ability to think clearly. I have also discovered that bipolar disorder is a lifelong condition. Mood swings are managed with a treatment plan, oftentimes including medication and counseling.

I have questioned if my husband really wanted to make me pay that day or if he was having a manic episode the entire time, starting from the moment I woke him up that morning?

I have also pondered whether Reggie's treatment of me all those years a result of a mental illness that was never treated. Was he really that controlling, manipulative, and malicious? The more I read, the angrier I became at his parents.

My anger slowly began to turn to hatred and it was starting to affect me. I knew that I needed to forgive my former in-laws for not getting Reggie the help he needed as a child. This forgiveness wasn't for them, it was all for me.

Dr. Jeannita Bussle

"It isn't the strength of your belief in healing that heals. Healing comes from a powerful God responding to your belief and trust in Him."

~ T.D. Jakes

Eight

Healing

When I received Reggie's death certificate and saw the word "suicide," my heart dropped. I had to submit his death certificates to so many entities to claim funds owed to me. All I could do was pray. I thought to myself that my children and I should not have to suffer because of Reggie's poor choice. We did nothing wrong and did not deserve to have our lives turned upside down even further because of something outside of our control. Within weeks I started to receive phone calls from insurance agents stating that our policies did not cover suicide, but God showed up.

The main policy that I was waiting to hear news of went through. Not only did my children and I keep everything, including our home, but we are also completely debt-free. My children will never have to pay a dime for school because they each have fully-funded college savings accounts. I met with my attorney and a financial planner to ensure that I invested wisely. My children and I are blessed beyond our wildest dreams because God showed up for us.

When the news spread of Reggie's death, some people whispered that I would get nothing and expected me to crash. As time went on, these same people could see that nothing was changing. How was it that I appeared to be doing just fine considering Reggie's cause of death? How was it possible that I walked under water and didn't get wet? There were people that stuck around just long enough to see if I would crash. When that didn't happen, and they realized all was well with me financially, I never heard from them again. My Pastor once said, "Beware of those that come running to provide counsel or comfort when going through a rough time. Some people bring food to your house just to see your furniture." Another part of my healing process has been using my God-given discernment in every area of my life, especially in my associations.

Unfortunately, there are some people in this world that are willing to lend their support during times of turmoil and trouble; however they are incapable of celebrating victories. My lifestyle was never upgraded after Reggie's death. I live in the same house in the same neighborhood. The sad reality is that people tend to pocket watch instead of focusing on what is important. This is especially true in the social media driven society we live in today. Online lurkers will examine everything you post better than the Federal Bureau of Investigation.

I have to give Reg credit because while he was alive, he would always tell me to be careful of what I posted on Instagram because people pocket watch. He and I differed in our beliefs on this matter. I always felt like I didn't care what people thought. My position was that I shouldn't have to hide what I have to make someone else feel better, but out of respect for Reg, there were certain things that I would not post on my account.

Once he passed, I posted what I wanted, and whenever I wanted. I have never been the type to boast; however, I have never felt the need to go out of my way to hide the things I have whether it be in a picture or in person.

Handbags, shoes, clothes, luxury cars, and big homes won't impress someone that is used to having it. To me it wasn't a big deal. However, Reggie was right all along about pocket watchers. What is even more disheartening is that some men will hate on a female worse than other women. Rather than be happy that my kids and I were doing well, the focus was on what I had. Rather than focusing on the fact that RJ and Jordyn were thriving in various activities, the focus seemed to be on me and the latest designer bag I carried. Rather than asking if my children were doing well emotionally, the question was, "How was I able to keep my home?" One thing I will never do is apologize for being blessed. Would it have been better if we were struggling? Only a sick individual could answer that question with a yes. If I am struggling, so are my children; whatever affects me affects them. I thought it was shameful that to a handful of people, the fact that I was living an abundant life made them feel uncomfortable.

Conversations that I used to have with my father never left me. He used to tell me that I have to watch even those closest to me, and that everyone isn't happy for me. Both my parents have always said, "Jeannita, everyone wasn't raised like you." They taught me never to be too trusting of anyone and to never reveal what all I really knew. Even when people talk behind your back, act like you don't know, but treat them accordingly. If you listen closely, people will always reveal how they really feel about you. A snake can only hide for so long.

People always want your glory, but don't know your story. They want the gain without the pain. I went through a lot and at the end of it all, God said, "Enough." God did not allow me or my children to suffer any more than we already had. He was with us all along. Our battles are fought in the spiritual realm and God took care of us.

My healing process has been slow, yet progressive. I have an awesome support team around me and many prayer warriors that constantly lift me up. However, there was one person left to forgive that could never say, "I'm sorry." I was angry at Reggie for so many reasons. Each time I took a step forward on my journey to forgive him, I took a step backwards.

I immediately got RJ in grief counseling with a licensed professional counselor that I knew personally. Many of his sessions were one-on-one; however, the first few were for both parent and child. Listening to my child express his feelings about his dad or watching him draw pictures of things he missed about his father helped RJ, but it infuriated me each and every time. Every time we sat in grief counseling, I would listen in disgust thinking about how uncalled for all of this was. I would think about how selfish Reggie was to do this. He was willing to hurt his own children all for the sake of getting even with me.

It took a lot of prayer for me to get to the place where I could even fathom forgiving Reginald. It was a process. Unlike all the other times, there will never be an apology from him. There will never be a bouquet of flowers waiting for me by the sink when I wake up with an apology note attached. There will never be a gift coming with a funny note to make me laugh. I eventually came to realize that Reggie apologized to me a lot in the past, but he never changed. An apology without change is simply manipulation.

My healing came when I accepted the fact that the man speaking to me that day was not my husband. Reggie left me feeling like the ultimate failure and he knew my past struggles. The man I loved would never intentionally scar me with a wound so deep.

I firmly believe mental illness is real. If it is left untreated it can and will ruin lives. As a school academic and guidance counselor, I know there are people with mental illnesses that learn to cope just enough to get by with day to day life. These people often suffer in silence or they unleash on those that love them the most. I believe that this was the case with Reggie.

I remember asking Reggie to attend marriage counseling on more than one occasion, but he refused because he thought it was unnecessary. Reggie was simply never taught coping skills needed for his internal struggles. Through prayer I realized that I could not continue being so angry at someone that was a victim himself. I could not be angry at someone that didn't realize he had a problem. In my heart I truly believe that my husband had an untreated mental condition that became progressively worse over time.

I made the choice to remember the nineteen-year-old I met at Tennessee State University who was loving, kind, funny, and gentle with me. I don't know who the man was that I woke up that August morning, nor do I know the man that had me walking on eggshells for years in my own home. My healing has been my choice and I choose to remember the good in Reggie.

I give God all the credit for moving me past being told, "This is all your fault," by my own husband before he committed suicide. I would not wish this on my worst enemy. It took a lot of prayer, fasting, yoga, and meditation to heal. I can now say that I finally did what I thought would be impossible. I forgave Reggie.

I occasionally get asked if I miss Reggie. I sometimes do. I miss everything good in him and about him. I miss my friend and companion. I miss watching him playing with our children and hearing them yell, "Daddy!" in excitement when he came home from work. I do not miss the emotional and verbal abuse. I do not miss waking up each day not knowing what to expect in terms of his mood. I do not miss feeling like nothing I did was ever good enough.

One thing I know for certain is that God is real. It is by his grace that I am here. I have read and seen stories on the news covering murder-suicide as a result of domestic disputes. This incident has taught me to see the positive in everything. Although I do not agree with what Reggie did and I wish things had turned out differently, I am so thankful that there were not four caskets.

My life is peaceful. I have supernatural peace that surpasses natural understanding. This type of peace only comes from God, especially considering the circumstances. My home is peaceful. My children are peaceful. I am peaceful. My faith allows me to believe that Reggie is also at peace. He had accepted Jesus Christ as his Lord and Savior. As a Christian, I have no doubt that Reg also has the supernatural peace that he longed for.

Being truly happy is something that I would not trade for the world. When you experience real peace you exude happiness. There have been people that have actually appeared offended because I did not grieve to their liking. They expected me to be all torn up, but prayer works.

Sorrow to Shero

"Peace is the most powerful weapon of mankind"

~ *Mahatma Gandhi*

Nine

Today

It has been three years since the passing of my husband and I can honestly say that my children and I are excellent.

RJ and Jordyn are doing exceptionally well. RJ is in the fifth grade and he is still in general education. I am thankful for early intervention. He continues to receive speech and behavior therapy and he thrives both in school and out of school. RJ loves basketball, swimming, and is a red belt in karate. My mother and I have made it our mission to ensure that he has the same abilities to succeed as every other child. I was determined not to let an autism diagnosis define him and it has not. RJ has friends and he is loved by all those that come in contact with him. He will occasionally mention his dad, but those times are few and far between. Grief counseling helped him tremendously. RJ is a happy child and I am grateful.

Jordyn is the diva of the house and literally runs my life. She is now in first grade. Ms. Jordyn loves her dance classes every Saturday morning. She also loves swimming lessons and she is an orange belt in karate. Jordyn can point out her dad in a picture, but unfortunately she does not remember him. Unlike her brother, she never asks me about him. When Reg passed away, Jordyn had just turned three years old. She is a spitting image of her father, but she has my personality. Jordyn is outgoing and very assertive with her many friends. She is little miss popular.

My prayer for my children is that they grow up fulfilled. I do not want them to have a hole in their heart because of their father's absence. We live in a very family-oriented neighborhood and most of the children around them live in two parent households. My children are attentive and I know they realize their family dynamic is different. I keep them in church and we pray together as a family. My mother has been instrumental in giving them both a strong spiritual foundation and talking to them about Jesus. We both pray for them, over them, and we keep them in church faithfully.

One of my fears has been that when they get older and discover what happened with their father, they might blame me. This fear came to an end one day when RJ heard me crying in my room and walked in. He flat out told me, "Stop crying, Mommy. You didn't do anything wrong." RJ is always in tune with me emotionally and he always checks on me. I'm not sure what made him say those words to me, but he did. God knew what I needed to hear at that moment and he used my baby to deliver that message.

I want my children to be proud of me. I want them to know that I did everything that I could to keep our family together. In the end, RJ and Jordyn gave me the courage to finally leave. I refused to let them grow up watching their mother being mistreated. I want my children to be able to say that their mother was their shero.

As for me, my focus since August 2017 has been on God, my children, my career in education, and completing my doctorate program. I began a doctoral program for educational leadership in January 2017, just eight months before Reggie's death. I never stopped. In fact, the morning of his viewing I was up bright and early posting an assignment to Blackboard from my phone. I eventually completed my program. I am now Dr. Jeannita Bussle. Glory to God!

I purchased my first investment property on my own in 2019. With the assistance and mentorship of my property manager and agent, I have been very successful. My attorney set up Shero Management LLC on my behalf for the purpose of real estate and self-publishing.

I am also a faithful yogi. I have been practicing yoga for four years and I enjoy every minute of it. Yoga keeps my mind and my body strong. Meditation and my faith in Jesus Christ have given me the calmness I need to weather the storm. My experiences have also helped me to learn a lot about myself. I now realize how important it is to not be judgmental. Never in a million years did I ever think that I would be writing this story - yet here I am. I have had plenty of fights from elementary to high school, but I didn't have the fight in me to stand up to one man. It is not until we are faced with certain obstacles that we realize who we truly are.

Although I displayed weakness for several years during my marriage, I am a lot stronger than I ever realized. I know now that I was always good enough regardless of how I was made to feel. I have finally accepted that none of this is or ever was my fault.

The realities of life have not only taught me about myself, but have also shed light on those around me. Some people have left my life and honestly, I am grateful. As a grown woman that has dealt with real life issues, I am very guarded in terms of who I trust. I am at a place in my life where peace has priority, so I can only tolerate genuine people in my circle, especially considering what I have dealt with. I believe that not everyone that leaves our lives is a loss, whether they are friends or family.

My loyal friends and family have been my rock. They have been an escape for me and they are the ones that have helped me to get through this ordeal. For the first time in my life I can truly say that my entire circle is solid. Instead of gossiping about my personal business, my people use their voices to speak life into me. I do not feel like I am the topic of discussion when I leave their presence. Each and every one of them will defend me in my absence and celebrate me in my presence. They have been the confidants that I have called on to vent and cry.

I am also blessed to still have a relationship with Reggie's extended family. I realize it has been difficult for them to comprehend what their nephew and/or cousin did. They will always have a place in my heart for their kindness and love towards RJ, Jordyn, and myself. We will always love them, and they will always be family.

Although I have forgiven my former mother-in-law and former father-in-law, I have not let them back into my life. I strongly believe that just because you've forgiven someone doesn't mean you have to have fellowship with them again. Toxic is not what is best for RJ and Jordyn, nor will it ever be.

My experiences have taught me to never put all my trust in man. People can change in an instant. Circumstances can change in an instant. As the late

Nipsey Hussle once said, "You can't possess people, you can only experience them." I experienced a man named Reginald Bussle. Through him, I experienced marriage, I am continuing to experience motherhood, and as a couple we experienced so many other firsts together. Through it all I am still grateful for all of the wonderful memories he and I shared. Those memories are what I try to focus on when thinking of my experience with Reginald.

The lesson here is that life has a way of humbling us. As I learned as a young girl, one event can turn your entire life upside down, but God never changes. He never leaves. He is faithful. He is true. One experience with God will forever change your life. Make sure you get to know Him.

About the Author

Dr. Jeannita Bussle has been a public-school educator for over fifteen years. Her expertise includes STEM education, socio-emotional learning, and college and career readiness. Dr. Bussle's passion is to give others hope and empowerment by sharing her testimony. She believes that one reason God allows us to experience obstacles is so we may help others make it through.

Her education includes a Doctor of Education in Educational Leadership K-12 and a Master of Education in School Counseling from Dallas Baptist University. She also earned a Master of Arts in Teaching Secondary Education from the University of Michigan-Dearborn, and a Bachelor of Science in Computer Science from Tennessee State University.

Dr. Bussle is the proud mom of two amazing children. Being a mother is her first priority and greatest accomplishment.

For more information, please visit Dr. Bussle's website:
www.drjbussle.com

Made in the USA
Coppell, TX
15 July 2020

31064325R00074